Discovering Patterns

© Aladdin Books Ltd 1998
Produced by
Aladdin Books Ltd
28 Percy Street
London W1P OLD

First published in the United States
in 1998 by
Copper Beech Books,
an imprint of
The Millbrook Press
2 Old New Milford Road
Brookfield, Connecticut

Project Editor: Sally Hewitt

Editor: Liz White

Design
David West Children's Book Design

Designer: Simon Morse

Photography: Roger Vlitos

Illustrator: Tony Kenyon

Printed in Belgium

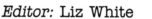

Library of Congress Cataloging-in-Publication Data
King, Andrew, 1961-
Discovering patterns / by Andrew King; illustrated
by Tony Kenyon.
p. cm. — (Math for fun)
Includes index.
Summary: Explores patterns in nature and in
numbers through games and projects using codes,
algebra, and arithmetic.
ISBN 0-7613-0734-6 (pbk.). —
ISBN 0-7613-0724-9 (lib. bdg.).
1. Number theory—Juvenile literature.
[1. Number theory. 2. Mathematical recreations.]
I. Kenyon, Tony, ill. II. Title. III. Series: King,
Andrew, 1961- Math for fun.
QA241.K56 1998
512'.7—dc21   97-41604
                               CIP AC

MATH *for fun*

Discovering Patterns

Andrew King

COPPER BEECH BOOKS
BROOKFIELD, CONNECTICUT

CONTENTS

INTRODUCTION

Everywhere you look there are patterns. The patterns on a butterfly's wings and in a spider's web are natural patterns. There are amazing patterns in mathematics too but you sometimes have to look quite hard to find them. Number patterns can help you to find the answer to all kinds of problems.

Try out the amazing activities, practical projects, and fun games in this book and you can discover how to find patterns in numbers and nature and learn how to use them.

● Follow the STEP-BY-STEP INSTRUCTIONS to help you with the activities.

● Use the HELPFUL HINTS for clues about the experiments and games.

● Look at MORE IDEAS for information about other projects.

 Yellow squares mean this is an easy activity.

 Blue squares mean this is a medium level activity.

 Pink squares mean this is a more difficult activity. You'll need to think hard!

NUMBER PATTERNS

You can find patterns everywhere in numbers. Even numbers can be divided in two without leaving any remainder. Squared numbers are made by multiplying the same number by itself, 3x3=9. There are many other strange and beautiful **number patterns**, some of which you will find out about in this book!

KEYPAD CRISIS

Play this with a friend.

1 Oh no! You have been locked out of your spaceship and you need to get back inside! You need to press numbers on the keypads to let you back in, but some of the numbers are missing.

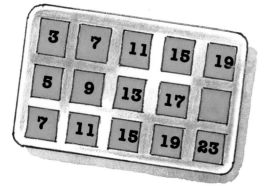

2 Luckily all the numbers are laid out in patterns. But what are they?

3 Some keypads have more than one number pattern. How many can you find?

4 Look along the rows of numbers, up and down, and from corner to corner. You may be able to find more than one number pattern on the keypad. One player closes their eyes and the second player covers one number on each keypad.

HELPFUL HINTS

● Some patterns are easy to follow. You can often figure them out by counting forward or counting backward. Which numbers come next in these sequences?

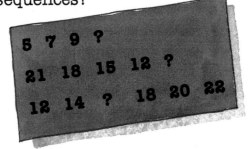

5 7 9 ?

21 18 15 12 ?

12 14 ? 18 20 22

● To find the missing number you needed to spot the number pattern.
● In these sequences there was a pattern of odd numbers, one which counted down in threes and one of even numbers counting up in twos.

MORE IDEAS

● You can make the keypad game more fun by hiding three or more numbers on each keypad.
● Try drawing your own keypad and making your own number patterns. If you are designing a pad to play against an adult, see how difficult you can make it!

5 The first player opens their eyes and tries to figure out which number has been hidden.

PATTERNS IN MULTIPLICATION

Knowing multiplication facts is very helpful when you are trying to solve some number problems. There are number patterns in multiplication that can help you remember your tables. You can also use your tables to make beautiful patterns.

SPIROLATERALS

1 You can make spirals with multiplication tables called spirolaterals. It helps to have some graph paper, but if you are careful with a ruler and a pencil, that will work too. Choose a multiplication table.

2 How about the six times table? Add up the digits in each number. Have you noticed a pattern?

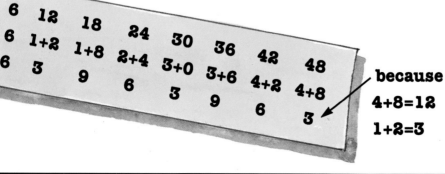

6	12	18	24	30	36	42	48
6	1+2	1+8	2+4	3+0	3+6	4+2	4+8
6	3	9	6	3	9	6	3

because
4+8=12
1+2=3

3 If you get a two-digit number when you add the digits together, keep adding them until you get a single-digit number.

4 Draw the first line 6 squares long then make a **right-angled** turn. The length of the next line is 3. Turn in the same direction again. The next is 9. Keep following the pattern until the lines start to retrace themselves. You could color in the patterns with colored pencils

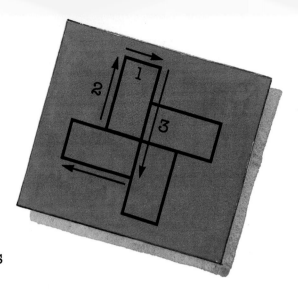

5 Try doing the same with other multiplication tables. Do any look like these?

MORE IDEAS

● Tear the corner off a piece of cardboard. Draw a straight line from the corner to the torn edge. Cut along the line. Mark the top corner with an "x," mark points from the tip at 1, 2, and 3ins along the edge you have cut. On a plain piece of paper draw a line 2ins long. Place the cardboard along the line with corner "x" at one end. Draw a line 1in long back down the edge of the cardboard (using the measurements). Then rest your piece of cardboard along the line you have drawn with the marked corner at the end. Draw back 3ins along the measured edge. Repeat these three steps over and over until you have made a pattern like the one on the left.

TRIANGULAR NUMBERS

Look at this number pattern

1   3   6   10   15...

What do you think comes next? This sequence is part of a special pattern called triangular numbers. To find out why they are called triangular numbers see page 30. It is made by adding consecutive numbers like this:

1 → 1+2=3 ——→ 1+2+3=6 ——→
1+2+3+4=10 → 1+2+3+4+5=15

Use this pattern to advise the government of Metropolis!

HIGHWAY MADNESS

1 The government of Metropolis has decided to build highways to link their seven cities. Because they are worried about the environment, they make a rule that every city must be linked directly to every other city by only one road.

How many roads need to be built?

2 Start by drawing two cities. How many roads need to be built to link them? Now draw three cities. How many roads would need to be built now?

3 Without drawing out the highway system, predict how many highways would need to be built for the seven cities in Metropolis.

4 Now mark them out and join them all with roads. Has the government of Metropolis made a good policy decision? What advice would you give to the government?

HELPFUL HINTS

● First find out how many roads need to be built with a smaller number of cities – say 3, 4, and 5. Look at the pattern of the triangular numbers on page 30. Three cities need three roads (1+2=3). Four cities need six roads (1+2+3=6). You can use the triangular pattern to figure out how many roads five cities would need.

MORE IDEAS

● Another interesting puzzle like Highway Madness is the handshakes problem. If you have eight people in a room and they all want to greet each other by shaking hands, how many handshakes will there be?

● You could start by figuring out how many handshakes you would need for a smaller group – as you did with the roads in Highway Madness.

LETTERS AND NUMBERS

In mathematics letters are sometimes used to represent numbers. This branch of mathematics is called **algebra**. It is a useful way of solving problems when you don't have any numbers to help or you are not sure what the numbers might be. Sometimes the numbers can be found out, then they can be substituted into a formula. In other words, they are swapped over for some of the letters.

NAME NUMBERS

 1 If a=1, b=2, c=3, and d=4, what do x, y, and z equal?

A N D R E W is worth 65 points because

A=1 N=14 D=4 R=18 E=5 W=23

1 + 14 + 4 + 18 + 5 + 23 = 65

 2 How many points is your name worth?

Think about the names of friends. Whose name do you think is worth the most points? Is it the name with the most letters?

NICOLA = 54

3 Do you have a "twin?" – someone whose name scores the same number of points as yours?

SIMON = 70

HELPFUL HINTS

● When you are figuring out how much your name is worth, it is helpful to set all the letters of the alphabet out in a table so you can quickly look up their value.

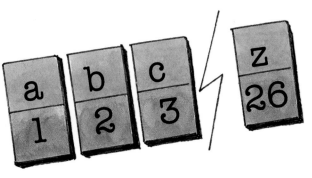

● When you are adding up a lot of numbers, it is easy to make a mistake. Check what you have done. A calculator can be useful.

MORE IDEAS

● The title of this page is "Letters and Numbers." It is worth 210 points. Can you make a sentence that is worth 200 points? How close can you get?

Can you score 300 points from a 17-letter sentence?

OPERATIONS AND FUNCTIONS

A function is when +, −, x, ÷, or other operations are used to change numbers. A **function** is a little like a machine in a factory that processes, or changes, something into something else.

NUMBER CRUNCHERS

1 You are the new engineer in the factory. You can see how the machine below works because the machine's functions are clearly labeled on the outside. When the 3 goes in, a 7 comes out because the function inside is x2 and then +1.

2 Unfortunately not all the machines are as clearly labeled. But you discover that if you put a number in a machine, it still gets crunched and changed.

Test the machine a few more times. What would happen if you put a number 6 in? What about 23? Try some other numbers and see what happens.

3 Try finding out the function for this number cruncher!

$4 \rightarrow$? ? $\rightarrow 12$

Which functions do you think were used in the big machine to turn the 2 into a 4? Can you think of any other way of doing it?

HELPFUL HINTS

● If you get stuck, try out a few operations in the machines and see what happens when you put a number in. Look for a pattern.

● If you are really stuck here are some clues:

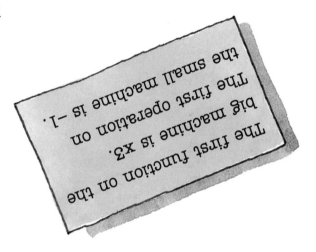

The first function on the big machine is ×3.
The first operation on the small machine is − 1.

MORE IDEAS

● Make up your own number cruncher machines. You could have more than two operations in each machine! Figure out some inputs and outputs, then see if a friend can solve your puzzle!

$2 \rightarrow$ +? −? ×? ÷? $\rightarrow$?

5 THINK OF A NUMBER

In algebra, when letters are used in calculations they could mean anything! But we can still work with them. If we do not know what a number is we could call it "n." Here is a trick that will work with any number. Try it out on your friends.

n

+6

x3

-18

Divide by the number you first thought of.

NUMBER RECYCLING PLANT

1 This is a way of calculating with any number and changing it using lots of different operations – adding, multiplying, dividing, and subtracting – and always arriving at the same result!

2 Your friends may need a calculator and a pencil and paper to help them.

3 Now say to your friends, "This truly remarkable trick can magically transform any number into a beautiful single one! Yes, it is true!"

HELPFUL HINTS

- Make sure you remember the number you started with. It helps to keep a note of your calculations.
- This could be recorded in a table:

n	+6	x3	−18	Divide by original number		−2
5	→11→	33→	15 ——————	÷5 ——————	→ 3	→ 1
11	→17→	51→	33 ——————	÷11 ——————	→ 3	→ 1

- Can you see now how the trick works?

4 Choose a number from one to a hundred, follow the operations, and presto!... one.

MORE IDEAS

- If you divide any number by itself, the answer is always 1. 7÷7=1, 5÷5=1, 59÷59=1, and 123÷123=1. Try doing the same with another number.
- Now you know how the magic works, try to make your own trick using many different functions that can turn numbers into ones.
- What happens when you divide or multiply a number by 0? Could you use this in your trick?

NUMBER CODES

We are so used to counting with the numerals 0123456789 and using the decimal system that they seem timeless, as though they have always been there. But they haven't! Different cultures have used a variety of **counting systems** and numbers.

Some of these can still be seen in regular use. Have you seen any Roman numerals? Letters are used to represent the numbers.

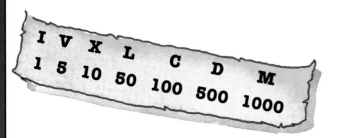

I 1 V 5 X 10 L 50 C 100 D 500 M 1000

The Mayan people lived over 2,000 years ago. Their number system used twenties and ones. We need to decode the system to know what the symbols represent.

= 0   = 1   = 2   = 3   = 4

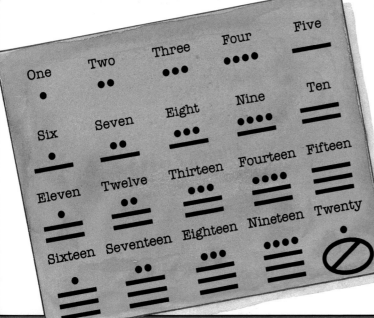

One •
Two ••
Three •••
Four ••••
Five ▬

Six
Seven ••
Eight •••
Nine ••••
Ten ▬▬

Eleven
Twelve ••
Thirteen •••
Fourteen ••••
Fifteen ▬▬▬

Sixteen
Seventeen ••
Eighteen •••
Nineteen ••••
Twenty ⊘

A number like 57 would be written like this...
because
2x20=40
+17=57

Twenties ••
Ones ••

NUMBER DISCOVERY

1 Imagine that you have been exploring uncharted land. You stumble across a stone tablet. There are some strange markings – they look like numbers.

This number is 28

=5   =6

=7   =8

=9

You eventually figure out what each symbol means.

2 What number do you think this is?

3 How would you write down 82? What about 56? Try 170!

Answer is 7 1 5

The system of counting was based on fives from — 19 and then in groups of twenty.

This symbol represented a zero.

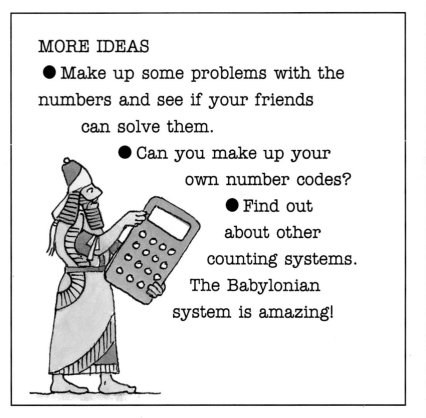

MORE IDEAS

● Make up some problems with the numbers and see if your friends can solve them.

● Can you make up your own number codes?

● Find out about other counting systems. The Babylonian system is amazing!

KNOW YOUR NUMBERS

The more you know about numbers the more patterns, links, and **connections** you will be able to make between them. What do you know about the number **25**? It is a square number, because **5x5=25**. It is a quarter of **100**. My uncle is **25** years old. It is an odd number. List everything you know about another number. How many connections can you make?

MYSTERY NUMBERS

1 The more you know about numbers the easier it will be for you to solve these number riddles. What are the mystery numbers and how are they all connected?

A solo spot for me. Odd and on my own. Who am I?

I had 10 subtracted and then I was multiplied by 2. That made 12. Who am I?

I can be divided by 12, 9, 6, 4, 3 and 2. If I am multiplied by 10 the answer is the same as the degrees in a whole turn. I am an even number. The product of my digits is 18. Who am I?

I was multiplied by 3 and then 3 was added. That made 30. Who am I?

The number of squares on a chessboard. 2 multiplied by itself six times. Who am I?

The sum of the first five odd numbers. An odd two digit number. Who am I?

The sum of my digits is said to be unlucky. I am not quite half a century. Who am I?

Add the sides of a square to the faces on a die and multiply by 10. Who am I?

I was divided by 9 and when 8 was subtracted, I was cut down to the size of just 1. Who am I?

The legs on most animals, tables, and chairs. Who am I?

HELPFUL HINTS

● With some of the mystery numbers you can work backward to find the answer by using the inverse or opposite operation. The inverse of x3 is ÷3.

The inverse of +6 is −6.

● For the problem "I was multiplied by 3 and then 3 was added. That made 30. Who am I?" you can begin from the 30. Work backward by subtracting 3, which makes 27 and then dividing by 3, which gives 9... the answer!

MORE IDEAS

● Make up your own mystery numbers! Think up your clues carefully and try them out on your friends. Remember to check your clues first!

MORE MYSTERY

To solve some problems you have to try to keep in mind a number of clues at the same time – simultaneously. In fact these are sometimes called simultaneous equations. They can be solved algebraically, but many simple ones can also be solved through trial and error. Try these!

COMBINATION CRACKERS

You have been on the trail of cunning criminals who have stolen some valuable jewels! A tattered, smudged piece of paper has been secretly passed to you with some clues that enable you to unlock the case holding the treasure.

1 The case has a four-digit combination lock and you only have a matter of minutes before the thieves return.

These are the clues...

The third digit is three more than the first.

The second digit is two more than the fourth.

All the digits add up to 17.

The second digit is three.

HELPFUL HINTS

- Stuck?! Then try to solve the problem using algebra. If the digits are a, b, c, and d, we know that $b=d+2$ and that $b=3$. So if $b=3$ then $3=d+2$ and therefore $d=1$.
- Use algebra to find out what a and c are. When the numbers you have chosen match all the clues then you have cracked the code and unlocked the case!

Answer is 5 3 8 1

MORE IDEAS

- If you found the first puzzle easy try this one!

You need to escape on a high-powered motorcycle, but it is chained up by, would you believe it, a four-digit combination lock. These are your clues for unlocking it...

- Why don't you find your own chain or case and make up your own clues!

The first number is one less than the fourth.

The sum of all the digits is fourteen.

The third number is twice as big as the first.

The fourth number is two less than the third.

The motorcycle answer is 3 1 6 4

MAN-MADE PATTERNS

People love patterns. Patterns can be seen all over the world on buildings, on furniture, clothes, and even on bodies. Have you seen any ancient Celtic knot patterns or those created by Islamic artists across the Middle East and North Africa? Perhaps you know of others. These designs illustrate many beautiful mathematical patterns.

SHONGO PATTERNS

This intricate pattern comes from Africa and is drawn by children on the ground in mud, clay, or sand.

1 The pattern is drawn in one continuous line. Your pencil should never be lifted from the paper. You can cross lines, but you should never go along the same line twice.

2 These are the first three patterns in the sequence. Try to draw them.

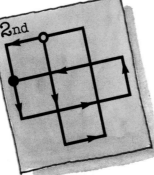

3 When you have drawn the first three try to draw the fourth. What about the fifth? Remember, your pencil should never leave the paper.

4 What patterns do you notice as you draw the shapes?

How long is the starting line on each of the new shapes? Count the squares covered by each shape. Can you see any number patterns?

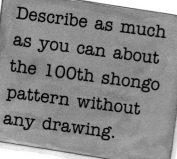

Describe as much as you can about the 100th shongo pattern without any drawing.

HELPFUL HINTS

● If you find it hard to get a sense of the pattern, trace over the shapes following the arrows on the lines carefully.

● It is a good idea to start drawing the patterns on graph paper. As you become more confident draw the shapes freehand on blank paper.

● After a little practice, you will be surprised how quickly they can be drawn.

● When you are looking for patterns, it is a good idea to note what you see in a table.

Shape	1st	2nd	3rd	4th
Perimeter	8	12	16	

MORE IDEAS

● This beautiful pattern comes from an ancient Celtic gravestone.

● Find some patterns from other cultures and try to draw them.

● What similarities or differences are there between the patterns you have found and the shongo pattern?

NATURAL PATTERNS

Nature is full of patterns. Next time you look at a plant or tree in your yard or park look at the curves, angles, and spirals that are formed. These patterns can be represented by numbers.

SPIRALS
You can draw many of these patterns by following a series of simple instructions.

1 Follow the instructions in Helpful Hints to help you make this circular grid. Starting from the center, move out to the first ring and mark a point.

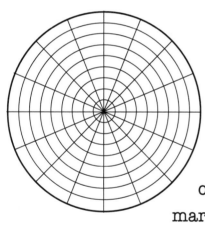

2 Lift your pen and move one section of the grid clockwise and out to the next circle and mark the point, join the points.

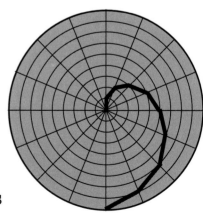

Keep moving out and clockwise one circle at a time, marking points and joining them.

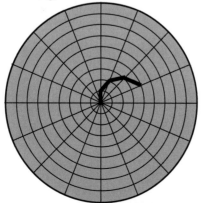

26

3 When you reach the outside circle, you will have made a curve.

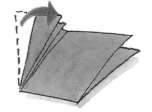

HELPFUL HINTS

● Find a piece of graph paper. Keep your compass point in the middle and draw 10 circles a half inch apart. Fold the paper in half and fold each side over and then over again.

MORE IDEAS

● Make another curve starting from the same center point. This time turn counterclockwise. You have drawn a beautiful leaf. Make lots of curves in a pattern on the same grid.

● Try other patterns. What happens if you move out two circles at a time?

● Try moving out one circle and turning two sectors.

● Other patterns can be made by following the grid lines and coloring in bright colors rather than just joining the points.

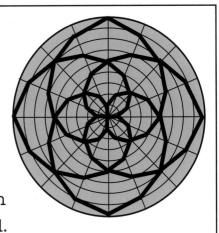

NATURAL NUMBERS

Nature can change simple number patterns into beautiful shapes. The Fibonacci sequence can be found everywhere in nature. Artists and architects have also used it in designs. It begins like this **1 1 2 3 5 8 13 21 34...** Can you see what the pattern is? The next number in the **sequence** is created by adding the previous two numbers, so the next number will be 21+34=55.

FIBONACCI FACTS

Did you know that the number of clockwise spirals on a sunflower head is 55 and the counterclockwise spirals is 34? Count them and check! Pineapples have 8 seeds arranged in a clockwise spiral and 13 in a counterclockwise spiral.

CURVE STITCHING

Other beautiful patterns can be made by adding numbers. For this project you will need a thick piece of cardboard. Draw out a cross on it.

1 On each arm of the cross mark five points 1 in apart. Mark the points on each arm with the numbers 1, 2, 3, 4, and 5. Pierce each point with a thick needle. Get an adult to help you with this.

2 Thread a needle with a long piece of yarn. Choose your favorite color. In one quater, stitch together the points that add up to 6, for example 1 and 5. When you have done one quarter, move on to the next with a different color yarn.

MORE IDEAS

● Try dividing **consecutive numbers** in the Fibonacci sequence. A

calculator is useful for doing this! Start by trying 8÷5=1.6. You will discover that the larger the numbers you divide, the closer you will get to approximately 1.618... This figure is known as The Golden Ratio. This ratio 1:1.6 has been used to design buildings like the ancient Greek Parthenon on the Acropolis.

● Take any four consecutive numbers in the Fibonacci pattern, for example 2, 3, 5, and 8. Multiply the two outside numbers (2x8=16). Multiply the two inside numbers (3x5=15). Subtract the second number from the first. Whichever four consecutive numbers you choose, if you follow this calculation, the answer will always be 1.

● Here is the sequence in reverse. What do you think comes next?

8 5 3 2 1 1 0 1 -1....

COMMON PATTERNS

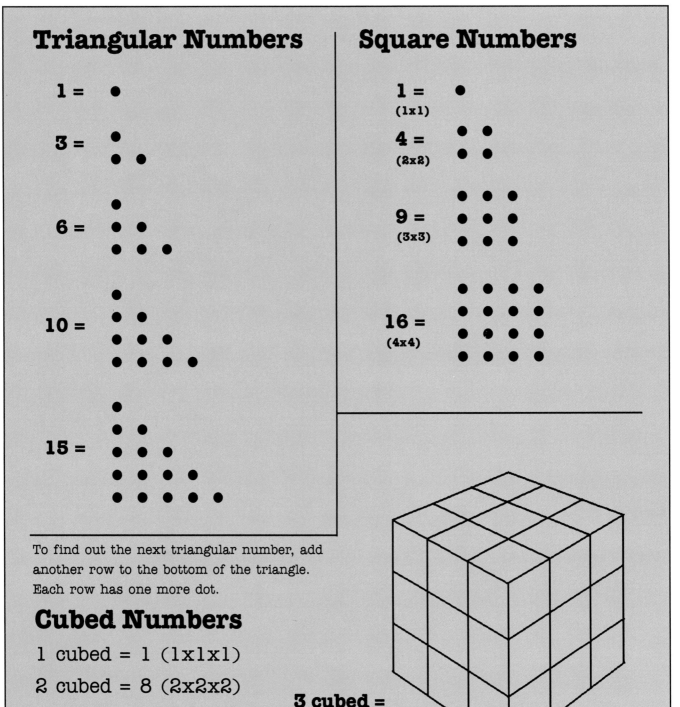

Triangular Numbers

1 = ●

3 = ●
   ● ●

6 = ●
   ● ●
   ● ● ●

10 = ●
    ● ●
    ● ● ●
    ● ● ● ●

15 = ●
    ● ●
    ● ● ●
    ● ● ● ●
    ● ● ● ● ●

Square Numbers

1 =
(1x1)
●

4 =
(2x2)
● ●
● ●

9 =
(3x3)
● ● ●
● ● ●
● ● ●

16 =
(4x4)
● ● ● ●
● ● ● ●
● ● ● ●
● ● ● ●

To find out the next triangular number, add another row to the bottom of the triangle. Each row has one more dot.

Cubed Numbers

1 cubed = 1 (1x1x1)

2 cubed = 8 (2x2x2)

3 cubed = 27 (3x3x3)

4 cubed = 64 (4x4x4)

3 cubed =

GLOSSARY

Algebra

In problem solving, letters are sometimes used to represent numbers or other amounts such as height or weight. This is useful when there are no numbers to help you or you are not sure what the numbers or amounts might be. This kind of mathematics is called algebra.

Angles

Where two straight lines meet, they make an angle. We can measure these in degrees. An angle of 90 degrees is called a right angle.

Connections

There are connections between numbers when there is something the same about them that makes a link between them. For example, a connection between the numbers 18, 60, and 36 is that they can all be divided by 6.

Consecutive numbers

Consecutive numbers are a list of numbers that follow one after each other without any missing, like this; 1, 2, 3, 4, 5, 6, etc.

Counting system

A counting system is a way of counting. Our counting system uses the numerals 0, 1, 2, 3, 4, 5, 6, 7, 8, 9.

Function

A function is a rule or a set of rules that are followed. A function could be "double the number and take 1 away," so the number 3 becomes 5 and the number 4 becomes 7.

Number patterns

Number patterns are formed when something is repeated again and again. For example, a number pattern can be made when a group of numbers are repeated like this – 2, 3, 4, 2, 3, 4, 2, 3, 4. Doing something to a number, such as adding 3 again and again, makes another kind of number pattern like this; 1, 4, 7, 10.

Perimeter

The boundary of a closed figure.

Sequence

A list of numbers such as 10, 9, 8, 7, 6, is a sequence because the same thing – in this case taking 1 away – has been done to each number in the list. Five will be the next number in the sequence because it is 1 less than 6.

INDEX